THE SOCIAL AND EMOTIONAL CHARACTERISTICS OF GIFTED STUDENTS

Tracy C. Missett

Cheryll M. Adams, Series Editor

National Association for Gifted Children
1331 H Street, NW, Suite 1001
Washington, DC 20005
202-785-4268
http://www.nagc.org

TABLE OF CONTENTS

INTRODUCTION

The social and emotional characteristics of gifted students
have been discussed and debated for decades both within
and beyond the field of gifted education. Too often in these
discussions, gifted children are conceptualized as
caricatures; they are understood to be EITHER exceptionally
well-adjusted emotionally and successful socially OR socially
isolated and emotionally maladjusted. Often these
competing stereotypes fail to recognize that gifted children,
like all children, experience emotional adjustment and social
successes in widely varying degrees over the course of their
development.

The purpose of this book is to illuminate and summarize
the broad range of emotional and social characteristics
gifted children display. Here, the emotional domain refers
specifically to the internal, psychological health and affective
features of a child as measured in terms of self-concept, self-
esteem, self-efficacy, resiliency, motivation, and task
commitment. The social domain refers specifically to
interpersonal skills as seen in the ways in which gifted
children interact with peers, parents, and teachers as
measured in terms of relationships and broad social skills.
The overall positive findings indicating that gifted children
are at least as well-adjusted or even more well-adjusted
both emotionally and socially are addressed first. The
unique vulnerabilities of gifted children who experience
relatively poorer emotional and social adjustment are
addressed next. The focus later is on current understandings
of how emotional and social characteristics are both
malleable and amenable to transformation over the course

of a child's development; and consequently, why these characteristics should be the subjects of purposeful nurturing and educational interventions. Finally, guidance is provided to parents and educators on promising strategies and curricula that are believed to promote positive emotional and social development for gifted students.

Note that many topics (e.g., self-perceptions, motivation, parenting, underachievement, twice-exceptional students, etc.) included here are not only broadly generalized, but themselves have a deep enough research base to warrant separate treatment. For those topics, additional resources are provided. Moreover, it is important to acknowledge that most of the research findings related to the social and emotional traits of gifted children are based largely on samples of predominantly Caucasian and middle to upper class children. Consequently, additional research is needed to conclude confidently that the research discussed here is applicable to the full diversity of children and across socioeconomic levels.

Notably, the gifted education literature often treats the terms "social" and "emotional" as unitary or parallel traits, with frequent references to the "socioemotional" or "social-emotional" characteristics of gifted children. Presumably, emotional and social traits are described as unitary because they often positively correlate. Nevertheless, the assumptions that social strengths necessarily correspond to high emotional adjustment while emotional difficulties must correspond with social deficits fail to recognize that, for some gifted students, social strengths do not always positively correspond to emotional well-being and vice versa. Thus, while they are often related, for our purposes the social and emotional domains are understood and discussed as distinct features of a child's overall personality.

DEFINITION OF GIFTEDNESS

Before any discussion of the emotional and social traits of gifted children begins, it is important to articulate one's definition of giftedness. While definitions of giftedness abound, and no single definition is agreed upon by all, Rena Subotnik, Paula Olszewski-Kubilius, and Frank Worrell[1] recently articulated a definition of giftedness based on a thorough examination of the relevant psychosocial research. According to Subotnik and colleagues, giftedness can be defined as follows:

Giftedness is the manifestation of performance that is clearly at the upper end of the distribution in a talent domain even relative to other high-functioning individuals in that domain. Further, giftedness can be viewed as developmental in that in the beginning stages, potential is the key variable; in later stages, achievement is the measure of giftedness. Psychosocial variables play an essential role in the manifestation of giftedness at every developmental stage. Both cognitive and psychosocial variables are malleable and need to be deliberately cultivated (p. 3).

The relevant psychosocial variables discussed by Subotnik and colleagues include (among others) ability, persistence, motivation, beliefs about self, resilience, and social supports. These variables are influenced by contextual factors such as school and family environments, economic stability, chance, and practice, all of which are subject to change over the course of a child's development. Because of its emphasis on the developmental nature of giftedness and thorough discussion of relevant research related to many of the psychosocial variables relevant to our discussion, this definition will be used.

THE EMOTIONAL STRENGTHS OF GIFTED STUDENTS

Meet Alyssa

Alyssa is an eighth grade student at Every County Middle School (ECMS). Alyssa was selected for inclusion in the Every County gifted program in third grade based on her ability and achievement test scores, which were all in the 99th percentile.

From the time she was a very young girl, Alyssa seemed to "have everything." She excelled in all of her classes, earning top grades throughout her elementary and middle school years. In fact, Alyssa skipped fifth grade and went directly to middle school from fourth grade. Her parents and teachers concurred that her social and emotional strengths, academic motivation, and tendency to socialize with older peers supported that decision. Alyssa sees herself as someone who can achieve almost anything she wants as long as she works hard, which she is determined to do. Her teachers enjoy the enthusiasm for learning and cooperation with peers she brings to the classroom.

By any standard, Alyssa would be considered a popular student. Alyssa's classmates have consistently elected her to student leadership positions, and she is captain of her soccer team. A group of friends constantly surround Alyssa at the lunch table, and most weekends she's at a sleepover. At the end of school year ceremony, Alyssa was voted "Best All-Around Student" by her teachers and classmates.

This summer, Alyssa plans to attend a camp offered by the Johns Hopkins Center for Talented Youth. She is confident that she will make friends and succeed academically while she is there. Nevertheless, Alyssa's parents are working with the school psychologist and gifted resource teacher to prepare her for camp attendance with other high achieving students to minimize any potential decrease in her perceptions of self as a highly competent student while she is at camp. When she enters high school in the fall, she plans to take Advanced Placement courses.

Terman's Longitudinal Studies

The vignette of Alyssa reflects the traditional conception of the highly confident, socially competent, and emotionally well-adjusted gifted student. The traditional notion that gifted students experience higher emotional and social adjustment when compared to typically developing peers is often credited to Lewis Terman, considered by many to be the father of research in the area of giftedness. In the seminal *Genetic Studies of Genius*[2] Terman conducted one of the first systematic studies of gifted students. His cohort of children had IQ scores of approximately 140 or higher. Terman commenced his studies in the 1920s and his participants were followed for over three decades. Over time, his research on Caucasian middle class children broadly showed that the children who participated in his study, in fact, became more professionally accomplished adults than the general population. In addition to their professional accomplishments, Terman's cohort also had more positive emotional outcomes over the course of their lives than comparable non-gifted individuals.

Reviews of research by Martin, Burns, and Schonlau,[3] as well as Subotnik and colleagues confirm Terman's findings that gifted individuals are at least as well as or more well-adjusted emotionally than their same age peers across multiple variables related to emotional health. Variables related to emotional health traits that have received significant attention in the field of gifted education include: self-concept, self-efficacy, self-esteem, motivation, resiliency, and giftedness as a protective factor. Each is briefly discussed.

Self-concept

Self-concept refers to a person's overall collection of perceptions about oneself, shaped through interaction with the environment and other people ("I am a likable/good person" and "I can get things done"). Self-concept is tied to personality, motivation, relationships with others, academic achievement, and patterns of behavior. Self-concept also depends upon one's developmental level and life experiences. Consequently, it often varies over the course of a child's life. In the educational realm, academic self-concept refers broadly to one's self-perception of academic competencies and abilities ("I am a strong student"). For gifted students, academic self-concept is typically based upon a process of social comparison whereby gifted students compare themselves to their peers using the class average as a frame-of-reference for assessing their own competence.

Gifted students generally exhibit higher or comparable self-concept when compared to same-age, non-gifted peers[4] with the academic self-concept of gifted students also tending to be more positive. This is particularly true in general education settings where gifted students tend to perform at a comparatively higher level. Positive academic self-concept for gifted students is associated with academic achievement, advanced coursework selection, intrinsic motivation, positive mental health, setting high educational goals, subsequent university enrollment and advanced degree attainment, and career development. In fact, the relationship between self-concept and achievement is reciprocal in that higher academic achievement generally is tied to more positive academic self-concept and vice versa.

Self-efficacy

Self-efficacy is an emotional trait related to self-concept. However, while self-concept relates to global beliefs about self ("I am a strong student"), self-efficacy refers to one's perceived competence in a specific task or in a particular domain ("I am an accomplished poet" or "I know how to study to do well on my test"). Overall, gifted students report comparable or higher levels of self-efficacy than their non-gifted peers. Like self-concept, positive self-efficacy is related to other desirable outcomes such as emotional health, motivation, perseverance, and higher academic achievement.

Self-esteem

Self-esteem refers to one's feeling of self-worth, self-confidence, and self-satisfaction ("I feel like I have much to be proud of" or "I feel like I am a person of worth"). Students with high self-esteem generally believe they can reach realistic goals as long as they put forth effort and persevere. Positive self-esteem is linked to many desirable academic and affective outcomes such as academic achievement, motivation, and positive emotional adjustment. Gifted students tend to experience more positive or comparable self-esteem when compared to same-age, non-gifted peers.

Self-concept, self-esteem, and self-efficacy each fall into the broader "self-perceptions" category. Because positive self-perceptions are so strongly tied to numerous desirable educational and affective outcomes, many educators and researchers including Subotnik and colleagues as well as VanTassel-Baska, Cross, and Olenchak[5] encourage targeted guidance and academic interventions over the course of a student's academic life to support the development of positive self-perceptions. Some of these recommended interventions will be discussed later.

Motivation and Task Commitment

Motivation is conceptualized as an overarching trait that encompasses many of the self-perceptions described above. It is broadly defined as a dedication to succeeding in one's activities ("I am determined to do well in school"). Motivation is typically broken down into two types: intrinsic (internal) and extrinsic (external) motivation. Intrinsic motivation refers to the desire to persist in an activity for its own sake, in other words for one's personal pleasure and/or curiosity. Extrinsic motivation refers to the desire to persist in an activity for an external outcome such as a grade or recognition from parents or teachers. Task commitment is conceived as a more focused form of motivation that enables an individual to persevere and work hard at a particular task ("I will spend as much time as I need to create an effective plan to reduce the bullying in my school.").

Together, motivation and task commitment facilitate the development of talents and abilities by enabling students to take advantage of talent-development opportunities and to engage in deliberate practice over time. It is only through deliberate and sustained practice and/or engagement that individuals, including gifted individuals, are able to transform ability into outstanding performance. Consequently, it should not be surprising that motivation, especially intrinsic motivation, and task commitment are strongly related to achievement.

Most gifted children show more motivation and task commitment, particularly intrinsic motivation,[6] than comparable non-gifted peers. This is particularly true for gifted children who understand that ability is malleable as an outcome of effort, who are in challenging academic environments, and who have social and academic peers of comparable ability and motivation. However, motivation and task commitment are often situation specific, follow a developmental trajectory, and can vary according to context. For example, a gifted student may be committed to preparing an excellent research paper on a topic of interest, but less motivated to study and do well on an algebra test. Or, a student may have been intrinsically motivated to perform well in elementary school due to a love of reading, but years later the same student might become more extrinsically motivated to get good grades and score well on high-stakes tests to gain admission to a select college. Or, a middle school-aged student may be motivated in an Honors Science class where there are other high achieving peers but not in a general education history class.

Like the self-perception characteristics, motivation and task commitment are amenable to development and nurturing. As a result, these traits, likewise, should be the subjects of direct academic and counseling interventions. Recommendations for the development of motivation and task commitment are offered later.

Giftedness as a Protective Factor

A growing body of research indicates that giftedness, particularly as defined by high intelligence (IQ >130) acts as a protective factor or "buffer" against emotional disorders. For example, Mueller[7] demonstrated that high intelligence confers emotional health advantages. The buffer provided by giftedness is indicated by findings showing that gifted students, overall, have fewer symptoms associated with (and lower rates of) depression, anxiety, and suicide ideation in comparison to typically developing peers. It is theorized that high intelligence may enable gifted students to utilize positive emotional traits such as resiliency and perseverance more efficiently and effectively to cope in stressful situations.

Additional protective factors such as well-established family, peer, and school support systems enhance emotional health outcomes for gifted students. Specific personality factors such as high self-concept, self-efficacy, self-esteem, and optimism also serve as protective factors and moderate emotional difficulties.

Resiliency

Another emotional health advantage conferred by high intelligence is resilience. Resiliency refers to the ability to overcome or survive and thrive against adversity and to be optimistic about the future. Thus, when exposed to adverse life experiences and conditions such as poverty or the loss of a close family member, highly intelligent children are often more resilient than typically developing peers exposed to comparable adverse conditions. One factor believed to contribute to a gifted child's ability to overcome adversity is the ability to attract the attention and support of adults and to have confidantes with whom burdens can be shared and ameliorated. As with many of the traits associated with gifted students, the ability to become resilient is viewed as a developmental process. As individuals have success in coping with and overcoming adversity, they typically can be expected to show gains in self-efficacy and self-esteem.

THE SOCIAL HEALTH OF GIFTED STUDENTS

In addition to the generally positive findings relating to emotional health, gifted students appear to be at least as or more socially adjusted when compared to same-aged typically developing peers. The overall social strengths of gifted students are evidenced by positive peer, teacher, and family relationships, in social self-concept, and broad social skills. Each is briefly discussed.

Family Relationships

Healthy family relationships and positive child-parent interactions are among the most important factors in the development of talent. Gifted students with positive parental relationships generally have higher achievement and more positive self-perceptions, achievement, motivation and task commitment, and overall social and emotional health. Thus, a gifted student's relationships with family members, along with the quality of their interactions, merit considerable attention.

The relationship between parents and their gifted children generally tends to be positive, and that such positive relationships support achievement. Research by Rudasill and colleagues[8] suggests this is true particularly where parents of gifted students employ a flexible parenting style that reflects high — yet reasonable and attainable — expectations for children, when parents maintain open lines of communication with their gifted children, and also accept the unique cognitive and emotional characteristics of their gifted children. Parents who enjoy strong and positive relationships with their gifted children more often encourage high academic performance for the purpose of learning rather than for the purpose of "being the smartest kid."

Overall, gifted children appear to receive a disproportionate amount of time and attention from their parents when compared to the amount of time and attention typically developing children receive. Many attribute this disproportionate attention to the fact that gifted children seek more input from parents and purposefully engage with them in conversation and activities more than other children. Perhaps as a result of the attention received, gifted students generally perceive that being gifted confers high social status with parents. Gifted children also typically have strong sibling relationships and they perceive that being gifted does not negatively impact relationships with siblings.

Teacher Relationships

There is little doubt that strong and supportive relationships between teachers and students are critical to academic achievement as well as social and emotional development throughout a student's academic life. Research by Gentry, Steenbergen-Hu, and Choi[9] confirm findings that for gifted students, the development of positive relationships with teachers is associated with higher academic achievement, motivation, and engagement, and has also been shown to reverse underachievement.

When considering the relationships gifted students have with their teachers, the research appears to be mixed. As reported by Robinson,[10] many studies support the view that teachers have comparable or more positive relationships with and dispositions toward their gifted students than they do towards typically developing students. Teacher relationships appear to be more positive with students who fit traditional conceptions of giftedness like Alyssa. Moreover, many gifted students report the belief that the gifted label confers high social status among teachers. They report feeling positively toward teachers who have domain expertise, enthusiasm in the classroom, a sense of humor and a respectful disposition towards gifted students. However, the student/teacher relationship tends to be less positive with students who do not fit the traditional conception of the "perfect" gifted student such as creatively gifted students and students with disabilities and from minority populations.

It is important to understand that teacher dispositions toward and relationships with gifted students often correspond to the amount of professional development teachers have received on issues related to gifted education. Thus, teachers who have direct experience and preparation related to the cognitive, social, and emotional characteristics and needs of gifted students tend to view gifted students more positively and have more positive relationships with those students. Thus, the National Association for Gifted Children (NAGC) Pre-K-Grade 12 Gifted Programming Standards[11] emphasize teacher development of a comprehensive understanding of the academic and psychosocial needs of gifted students. Similarly, gifted students perceive their relationships with teachers in gifted programs to be more positive than with teachers in the general education setting. Many gifted students also report that Advanced Placement (AP) and International Baccalaureate (IB) settings provide satisfying and positive emotional connections with teachers[12] to sustain them through the difficulties of challenging curricula, and teachers in these advanced programs likewise more often report having stronger relationships with their gifted students.

Peer Relationships

Friends are vital to the healthy social development of children as friendships help children learn to cooperate, problem solve, and communicate with others. Having friends at school has been shown to promote more positive attitudes toward school and to relate to increased academic motivation.

Recent research by Bain and Bell[13] confirm prior findings that gifted students generally perceive themselves to be socially accepted, able to make and maintain friendships, and to be well-liked by both gifted and non-gifted peers. Such positive perceptions persist through the middle school years. They also appear to be well-founded as gifted students tend to be at least as or more well-liked by both gifted and non-gifted peers. However, an exception appears in the case of gifted students with extremely high verbal abilities who perceive themselves to lack social standing. By high school, beliefs about social standing often change with some gifted girls perceiving that they are more popular if they are also pretty, and some gifted boys feeling more popular if they are also strong athletes. These developmental trends appear to be consistent with the evolving perceptions of non-gifted peers. Moreover, research shows that social standing does in fact improve for more athletic and attractive students.[14]

It is important that gifted students have friendships with other gifted students. The development of positive relationships with high achieving friends (as well as teachers and parents) is associated with higher achievement and the reversal of underachievement. Additionally, for those students experiencing trauma, poverty, divorce of parents, or other adverse life circumstances, supportive friendships with other high achieving peers have been shown to aid in the development of resilience.

Social Self-concept

Social skills refer to the set of skills people use to interact and communicate with others. Social self-concept refers to a person's collection of perceptions about the degree to which others like or wish to socialize with them ("People like to hang out with me"). As a whole, gifted students are well-liked by other people including their peers, with same-aged peers tending to view gifted students as having strong social skills. Moreover, gifted students tend to exhibit positive social self-concept and perceive themselves to be competent in social situations. Positive social self-concepts among gifted children also have been observed in high-ability classroom groupings. Additionally, most gifted students generally perceive that the gifted label either confers social status or does not make it harder to make friends. Thus, they typically feel socially accepted, report having close friendships, and feel interpersonal competence in making friends.

SOCIAL AND EMOTIONAL VULNERABILITIES OF GIFTED STUDENTS

Meet Edward

Edward is a seventh-grade student at ECMS. Edward was selected for inclusion in the county's gifted program as a third grade student based on his high verbal ability scores, which were above 160. Despite his exceptionally high ability score, Edward's grades in most subjects have been in the average range since he entered middle school. The exception has been math, where Edward is in advanced courses and achieves at a high level.

Edward has had difficulty "fitting in" from the time he started school. Edward is introverted and has difficulty making and keeping friends. Because he has a sense that he is different from and not popular with his peers, Edward tends to stick to himself at recess and lunch where he reads magazines about electronics and science fiction novels. Occasionally he eats lunch with his Math teacher who has taken an interest in Edward. He doesn't know any other children who share his interests. Most of Edward's classmates feel that he is a "dweeb." While a few kids tease him, most ignore him. Edward's parents worry that he will become the target of bullying. At home, Edward spends most of his free time building electronic prototypes.

When Edward has big projects due at school, he becomes so overwhelmed and worried that his work won't be perfect that he is unable to finish his projects. On occasion, his anxiety is so acute that he cannot go to school. As a result, Edward's parents have been taking Edward to a psychiatrist to help with his perfectionism and low self-esteem. The school psychologist and gifted resource teacher include Edward in a weekly peer journaling lunch group for gifted students. They also have worked with his parents to find opportunities for Edward to socialize with other high-ability students with similar interests. For example, Edward is enrolled in a robotics and video game programming summer camp with other students who enjoy electronics. In eighth grade, Edward will go to the high school to take an advanced math class.

The vignette of Edward reflects many of the emotional and social vulnerabilities associated with gifted children. As illustrated by this vignette, not all gifted students exhibit greater emotional adjustment and social assets than comparable peers or conform to traditional notions of the "perfect" gifted student. Rather, the psychosocial well-being of many gifted students is adversely impacted by a combination of internal and contextual factors including type of giftedness (e.g., profoundly gifted), a mismatch between cognitive and emotional development, poor educational fit, poor home and community environments, trauma, and a variety of personal characteristics such as low resilience and low self-perceptions. Below, some contextual factors frequently described in the gifted education literature are discussed.

Profoundly Gifted

While most gifted children experience positive social relationships, the degree of social difficulty a gifted child experiences appears to increase with the level of giftedness. This is most evident for highly and "profoundly gifted" students or, as described by Gross,[15] those with IQs at the 99.99th percentile and above. The lack of success profoundly gifted students experience in cultivating and developing social relationships can be attributed to the lack of same-aged peers with comparable intelligence or interests and the lack of peers with whom the profoundly gifted child can relate. Moreover, the social isolation and emotional difficulties experienced by profoundly gifted students increase in unchallenging academic environments. Consequently, profoundly gifted students tend to seek out the time and attention of adults and older children in lieu of same-aged peers. Profoundly gifted students also report that they are less likely to feel they make their parents happy and proud in comparison to more moderately gifted students.

If left in an unchallenging environment devoid of peers with whom they can relate intellectually, profoundly gifted children are at great risk for chronic social isolation, low self-concept and self-esteem, and academic underachievement. Acceleration of one or more grades and placement in more stimulating academic environments offer profoundly gifted students opportunities to achieve at high academic levels, to work and play with more comparable intellectual peers, to be valued as a classmate and friend, and to ameliorate the social isolation they experience in same-aged classrooms.

Asynchronous Development

In addition to being characterized as cognitively advanced, Silverman[16] further describes many gifted children as uniquely and intensely sensitive, perceptive, empathetic, and morally idealistic. However, the advanced cognitive development of many gifted children outpaces their ability to manage these intense emotional experiences. Because they develop asynchronously, the combined cognitive and emotional characteristics are "mismatched." This mismatch, in turn, causes some gifted children to experience the world in a qualitatively different way than their non-gifted peers, leaving many emotionally vulnerable. Thus, a parent or teacher may have a seven year old child who is reading at the 8th or 9th grade level who becomes emotionally overwhelmed by the loss of a favorite toy or who stubbornly refuses to share with a peer. For children who develop asynchronously, modifications in parenting, teaching, and counseling become necessary.

Big Fish Little Pond Effect

As indicated above, gifted students typically develop positive academic self-concepts when placed in general education and mixed-ability environments. However, the "big-fish-little-pond effect" (BFLPE) reduces academic self-concept for many gifted students in more homogeneous settings.[17]

BFLPE refers to the phenomenon where gifted students experience lower academic self-concepts when attending selective schools or participating in programs wherein the average ability levels are high. Because individuals typically use their peer group as a frame of reference for gauging their own academic competence, some gifted students who are at the top of their peer group in the general education setting become average or below average in more selective and homogeneous settings. Because the gifted student now perceives him or herself as comparatively less "gifted," self-concept declines in children vulnerable to the BFLPE. Thus, for some gifted students, attendance at selective schools or participation in gifted programs negatively impacts self-concept. The BFLPE has been seen in gifted students in the elementary grades through university level, in residential schools for gifted learners, as well as in summer programs for gifted students.

Not all gifted students are vulnerable to the BFLPE. Rather, a variety of individual and contextual factors can intensify or moderate the phenomenon. For example, students who do not have the option to pursue individual topics of interest in the homogeneous setting or who are more extrinsically motivated are likely to be more intensely impacted by the phenomenon. Moreover, highly anxious students or those who already have low self-esteem are more likely to experience the BFLPE.

The negative effects attributable to the BFLPE may ultimately prove to be minimal for many gifted students. First, the reduction in academic self-concept appears to be temporary for many students. Second, the BPLFE may ultimately cultivate pro-social and emotional adjustment in cases where gifted students experience a humbling adjustment toward more realistic perceptions of one's relative ability. Nevertheless, parents and educators of gifted children should be aware of the possible negative impact on self-perceptions that selective academic settings have, and they should be prepared to offer guidance to minimize and reverse any such impact.

The "Gifted" Label

As indicated in the previous section, there is not a strong body of evidence indicating broad-based biases against "giftedness." To the contrary, overall, being identified as gifted confers social status in most social and academic settings. Nevertheless, as Callahan and Hébert[18] as well as Assouline, Colangelo, and Heo[19] point out, in some contexts and for certain gifted students, giftedness is viewed as stigmatizing. For example, some gifted children harbor internal perceptions of being both different and exposed to peer rejection based on their gifted label, even if their own self-perception is to view their giftedness positively. Some gifted children become the target of bullying. In response to feelings of being stigmatized by the label, whether those feelings are accurate or not, some gifted children withdraw socially. Alternatively, gifted students feeling stigmatized might develop an alternative identify which masks their giftedness in order to conform and gain (or retain) acceptance.

The effort to mask giftedness occurs in school environments that embrace and cultivate conformity, and/or devalue giftedness in favor of other social or athletic outcomes. For example, Worrell[20] summarizes research describing the phenomenon of masking giftedness that has been observed among ethnically diverse and female gifted students. Specifically, some high-achieving African-American students report that participation in advanced coursework and doing homework can be associated with "acting White," whereas underachieving and downplaying high academic ability are associated with "acting Black." Acting White is viewed negatively and as a betrayal of ethnic identity whereas acting Black is viewed as belonging to and embracing ethnic identity. When social identity conflicts with academic identity, some minorities may be less willing to participate in gifted programs or achieve academically. However, it is believed that the social ostracism perceived and experienced by certain minority students can be moderated by the inclusion of a core group of other gifted students from the same minority group.

Gifted girls may choose to mask their giftedness if they perceive high intelligence to be a social disadvantage — such as making boys less attracted to or interested in them — or if they prioritize meeting the needs of others instead of pursuing areas of personal interest. There is also evidence that some gifted girls experience lower academic self-concept, self-efficacy, and motivation in science and mathematics as compared to gifted boys.

In addition, the gifted label leads some gifted students to become overly concerned with how smart they are perceived to be rather than with how hard they are working or how much they are learning. As Dweck[21] has suggested, the anxiety produced by such concerns can lead students to avoid engaging in academically rigorous programs and opportunities.

Finally, the label "gifted" may make some students reluctant to ask parents or teachers for assistance, based on the belief that they may be judged and found lacking in competence or intelligence for seeking help. Such beliefs may lead gifted students to disguise academic, social or emotional challenges for fear of disappointing important adults. When students conceal their difficulties, parents and teachers are more likely to miss indicators of distress and fail to obtain necessary supports for these students.

Underachievement

When students with demonstrated talents and potential do not perform at a level commensurate with their measured ability, or fail to take advantage of opportunities to develop their talents, they are said to be underachieving. The phenomenon of underachievement among gifted students has been a matter of longstanding concern to parents and educators. In fact, it is one of the most common reasons parents of gifted students seek counseling for their child. Factors that contribute to underachievement are numerous and varied. They include unchallenging academic environments, changes in the student's life circumstances (for example, moving or divorce of parents), lack of support from parents and teachers, trauma, perceptions that the gifted label is socially disadvantageous, and/or lack of intrinsic academic motivation. Gifted children with learning disabilities that impact their ability to achieve and demonstrate learning (known as "twice-exceptional" students) also experience (or are perceived to experience) underachievement particularly as the disability becomes more pronounced or becomes more problematic with increasing school demands. Underachievement is also typically seen in students with already low self-perceptions.

While the phenomenon of academic underachievement should be of concern to educators and parents, it can be reversed for many gifted students who will go on to resume academic success. For example, if the root cause of underachievement is an unchallenging academic environment or a change in life circumstances, underachieving students can become successful when the academic environment becomes more challenging or the life circumstance normalizes. Moreover, many of the factors initially contributing to underachievement like low self-perceptions are developmental in nature and amenable to counseling, mentoring, and support. However, for some gifted students underachievement becomes difficult to reverse when it persists for an extended period of time.

Perfectionism

Perfectionism, indicated by the need to avoid making mistakes, is a characteristic often associated with giftedness. For the majority of gifted students, perfectionism is an adaptive and positive characteristic that results in high-quality products. Linda Silverman[22] suggests that gifted students exhibit more adaptive manifestations of perfectionism than non-identified peers. Nevertheless, perfectionism becomes maladaptive and produces stress in many cases, sometimes to an acute and dysfunctional degree, when children do not feel their work is perfect. Students experiencing maladaptive or dysfunctional perfectionism suffer loss of self-esteem and typically experience other poor mental health outcomes (e.g., anxiety and depression). Others may procrastinate or avoid completing assignments altogether when they believe they will be unable to produce work that is perfect. Precursors to development of maladaptive perfectionism include parental and teacher emphasis on grades rather than learning, low self-concept, and chronic mental health concerns such as anxiety and depression.

Like many of the social and emotional traits already discussed, perfectionism is believed to be developmental and malleable. Thus, the development of adaptive perfectionism and amelioration of maladaptive perfectionism are amenable to counseling intervention. Counseling efforts designed to help gifted students develop more adaptive perfectionism through setting high but realistic personal standards and goals are recommended. Parents and teachers should also be counseled and encouraged to help students learn to achieve for the sake of learning rather than winning or being the best.

Relationships

Just as a gifted child's social and emotional adjustment can be positively impacted by their relationship with parents, the nature of this relationship can also adversely affect a child's social and emotional development. Children with parents who focus on their child's gifted label rather than on their accomplishments, or on performance goals rather than learning goals, tend to be less motivated, have lower self-perceptions, and experience poorer relationships with their parents. Moreover, when parents set low expectations and provide excessive flexibility and independence, their gifted child may feel adrift or unmotivated.

As described by Robinson,[23] not all teachers who work with gifted students enjoy strong positive relationships with them. Some teachers harbor negative attitudes toward gifted students and view them as self-centered and arrogant. Some teachers have more negative views of highly creative students, who are less conformist and more likely to question authority. Many teachers believe that gifted students do not need to persevere or put forth effort to achieve academically. Thus, when gifted students struggle in the classroom these teachers misperceive them to be lazy or acting out. Many teachers also have less positive perceptions of and relationships with gifted low income, minority, and twice-exceptional students who might not conform to traditional conceptions of giftedness.

As suggested above, negative perceptions held by teachers toward gifted students are amenable to change. Many teachers who held negative views toward gifted students show changes to more positive attitudes after participation in training in the social, emotional, and cognitive characteristics of gifted students. Thus, as recommended by the NAGC,[24] professional training to help teachers of gifted students understand the needs of a diverse range of gifted learners may help teachers better respond to their gifted students and, in turn, develop better relationships with them.

Low Income, Minority, and Twice-Exceptional Gifted Learners

Gifted students who are poor, twice-exceptional, and/or who come from minority backgrounds (e.g., African-American, Native American, Hispanic) have long been under-represented in gifted programs. While the research on gifted students from these populations is well beyond the scope of this work, several generalizations on their social and emotional health should be noted.

Worrell[25] and Nicpon, Rickels, Assouline, and Richards[26] point out that, broadly speaking, minority, low socioeconomic, and disability status are each correlated with increased risks of poor social and emotional outcomes including comparatively low self-perceptions, motivation, and academic achievement, as well as less stable family and peer relationships. In the gifted education setting, these risks are compounded because many of these students do not fit traditional conceptions of giftedness. Consequently, teachers are less likely to recognize their gifts and talents. This leaves many students in unchallenging academic environments that can exacerbate their social and emotional difficulties.

For gifted students with disabilities, the social and emotional health disparities are well documented. As demonstrated by Antshel and colleagues[27] as well as Nicpon and colleagues,[28] high IQ youth with Attention Deficit Hyperactivity Disorder (ADHD) appear to experience significantly higher rates of mood disorders, including depression, than high IQ students without ADHD. Thus, the protective effect of high intelligence may not exist or is moderated in the presence of ADHD. Gifted students with ADHD, Autism Spectrum Disorder (ASD), and emotional disabilities also tend to have lower perceived self-concept and self-esteem, as well as more difficulty with social relationships, in gifted (and regular) education classrooms and programs. As students with disabilities develop, they may gain insight into their social and emotional difficulties. For some, this increased self-awareness further produces anxiety as they become more aware of their social limitations. Academic and counseling interventions for twice-exceptional students that focus on development of strengths rather than solely on weaknesses are critical to their success in the educational environment.

PROMISING AFFECTIVE CURRICULA AND PROGRAMMING OPTIONS

Meet Ms. Alvarez and Mr. Johnson

Ms. Alvarez is as Social Studies and gifted education resource teacher at ECMS. Alyssa and Edward (students described in the vignettes above), as well as Sally (a student described in the vignette following) take honors history courses with her. Mr. Johnson is the school psychologist. Dr. Jones, the principal at ECMS, asked Johnson and Alvarez to develop an affective curriculum (called "The Social and Emotional Curriculum") that would address the broad range of social and emotional characteristics and needs of gifted students at ECMS. To help them accomplish this goal, Dr. Jones provided a variety of resources related to the social and emotional traits of gifted students, as well as appropriate strategies for addressing the unique needs of the gifted students at ECMS. (See Resources section.) Dr. Jones also sent Johnson and Alvarez to the Annual NAGC Convention to learn as much as possible about the social and emotional needs of their gifted students.

Following these professional development opportunities, Mr. Johnson and Ms. Alvarez recognized that the gifted students at ECMS experienced varied levels of social and emotional adjustment and that these students had a diverse range of needs. They also recognized that the social and emotional features of their gifted students were tied to their academic placements. Thus, their approach to developing and implementing the Social and Emotional

Curriculum was to differentiate both academically and psychosocially for the gifted students at ECMS.

Mr. Johnson and Ms. Alvarez first focused on academic differentiation and on ensuring that ECMS gifted students were placed in appropriately challenging courses. They noticed that the county had not supported the practice of acceleration for its most advanced students. Through a series of information sessions, webinars, flyers, and email alerts, they successfully encouraged teachers, administrators, and parents to more seriously consider the emotional and social benefits of acceleration for their most highly able students. Using the Iowa Acceleration Scale (IAS) (3rd ed.) to screen for academic, social and emotional (motivational) readiness, several students at ECMS and Every County Elementary were selected to skip one or two grades. Johnson and Alvarez also held several informational sessions for parents at which they discussed applications to and participation in regional talent search programs. For those students who were accepted, including Alyssa, Johnson and Alvarez held conferences with parents and students to discuss and minimize any adverse impact on emotional health that might arise from the BFLPE. Similar conferences were available for students (and parents of students) who were planning to participate in the county IB program upon entering high school.

In her history classes, Ms. Alvarez's students completed interest inventories and talent portfolios in order to integrate learning activities that engaged the explicit interests of her students. Through these materials, she discovered several students were interested in the global refugee crisis. Ms. Alvarez grouped these students in a research assignment where students were asked to report on and develop strategies for resolving international crises.

As part of their research, this student group visited the local International Red Cross office and interviewed the director and employees to inform their research presentation. Ms. Alvarez also located professionals in the community who could serve as mentors, such as the Red Cross director, for those students hoping to volunteer over the summer break.

Mr. Johnson began to host "peer support networks" during lunch hour and after school for students. The purpose was to provide a space for students who wanted the opportunity to discuss pressures they were experiencing in their lives and that affected their success in school. He encouraged students to join him in a nonjudgmental context where they would feel supported and less alone, where they could explore beliefs about what it meant to be "gifted," and where they could reframe difficulties into a problem-solving and social coping framework. During the luncheons, some students openly discussed their difficulties. Those who felt uncomfortable with open discussions often wrote in journals or scheduled individual meetings with Mr. Johnson to speak privately. He also helped the language arts teacher organize a bibliotherapy lunch group for students who wanted to think through goals and personal issues through literature and biography.

Educators naturally tend to emphasize the cognitive development of their gifted students. But as the vignette of Alvarez and Johnson illustrates, the social and emotional development of gifted students are essential educational outcomes that must be addressed to maximize learning and achievement. To that end, many in the field of gifted education including Subotnik and colleagues,[29] Nicpon and Pfeiffer,[30] as well as VanTassel-Baska and colleagues[31] recommend purposeful counseling and an affective curriculum specifically designed to promote the emotional and social health of gifted students. Some interventions and programs that have been recommended are discussed.

Acceleration

Many of the emotional and social vulnerabilities of gifted students arise in the context of, or are exacerbated by, unchallenging educational environments that do not allow students to progress at a pace suited to their readiness level. Consequently, acceleration is an academic intervention recommended for highly able students. Acceleration allows students to progress through educational programs at a rate faster than typical same-aged peers. There are many ways to accelerate a student. For example, students can skip one or more grades, and/or receive higher-level instruction in an advanced-grade classroom (e.g., advanced mathematics classes), and/or enroll in college courses during high school.

Although many parents and educators mistakenly believe that acceleration will harm students emotionally and socially, the research convincingly shows that most accelerated students show higher self-perceptions, higher interpersonal abilities, greater social leadership, higher educational aspirations and outcomes, stronger motivation, and more positive perceptions of peer relationships than non-accelerated gifted students. Based on this deep research base, Colangelo, Assouline, and Gross[32] published a two-volume report synthesizing decades of research on acceleration. This report identified the pro-educational, pro-social, and pro-emotional impacts of acceleration, and called upon educators to utilize the intervention more frequently for the most highly able students. To aid in the determination of whether a student is academically, emotionally, and socially appropriate for grade acceleration, the Iowa Acceleration Scale (IAS) (3rd ed.) is a tool often recommended to help schools and parents make effective and well-informed decisions regarding acceleration.

International Baccalaureate (IB) Diploma Program

The International Baccalaureate (IB) Diploma Program is a liberal arts college preparatory curriculum. Not only does the IB program mandate a rigorous academic curriculum, it also attends to many affective and social components of learning. Curriculum components cultivating cultural sensitivity, interpersonal development, problem solving, and social competence are included. Moreover, IB students undertake in-depth research into an area of interest through the lens of one or more academic disciplines. Because IB provides academic rigor and integrates student interests, it addresses many factors contributing to underachievement. It should be noted that some researchers including Hertberg-Davis and Callahan[33] have criticized the IB Diploma Program and Advanced Placement (AP) for their "one-size-fits-all" approach that does not accommodate the learning styles of traditionally under-represented students such as those who are twice-exceptional or come from low-income and ethnic minority backgrounds. To address these criticisms, the implementation of programs and interventions — such as support groups and intensive writing and academic skills training — is encouraged to better prepare these students for academic success in AP and IB programs.

Discussion Groups

Discussion groups have the potential to be an effective and significant strategy in an affective curriculum.[34] Led by trained educators or school psychologists and counselors, discussion groups provide a forum allowing gifted students to voice concerns and experiences in a non-judgmental context devoid of grades or performance measures.

Discussion groups also have the potential to encourage gifted students to share concerns with other gifted students, provide opportunities to connect socially with intellectual peers, learn about self, reduce anxiety, and improve self-perceptions. Care should be taken not to "create problems" or to suggest that it is inherent that to be gifted is to be faced with social or emotional problems.

Operation Houndstooth

Developed by Joseph Renzulli, Operation Houndstooth[35] provides a framework for developing and supporting socially constructive attributes in young gifted children through participation in civically and socially engaging activities. Operation Houndstooth addresses six components that relate to overall academic, social, and emotional success including: optimism, courage, romance with a topic or discipline, sensitivity to human concerns, physical/mental energy, and vision or sense of destiny. These components encompass many of the psychosocial variables discussed by Subotnik and her colleagues such as motivation, task commitment, resiliency, self-concept, and self-efficacy. Gifted students interact with and develop competencies in each of the six components through a vehicle called the Total Talent Portfolio (TTP). The TTP helps students gain insights into individual areas of strength and interest, the learning environments and type of interactions (peer, adult, etc.) they prefer, and their preferred modes of thinking and expression. Because students are themselves responsible for developing the TTP, they learn to take responsibility for their learning while gaining autonomy and simultaneously develop self-perceptions. They also are empowered to avoid unchallenging or uninteresting learning environments.

Emotional Intelligence Framework

Joyce VanTassel-Baska's Emotional Intelligence Framework[36] provides a structure for addressing both academic and affective components of a gifted program. The emotional intelligence framework emphasizes the components of self-assessment (helping gifted students understand their abilities in light of their personalities and interests), philosophy of life (defining what they believe and value), bibliotherapy (continued use of literature and biography to help students understand themselves through characters and role models), talent development plan (encouraging students to develop a personal talent plan and to monitor personal growth), and emotional intelligence (the ability to perceive and regulate emotions). Each component is purposefully targeted through lessons designed to develop problem solving and to encourage written and oral communication about emotional issues.

CONCLUSION

This publication broadly addresses a wide range of social and emotional traits gifted children typically exhibit. Specifically, it emphasizes the current understanding that gifted children are diverse in their emotional and social health, that social and emotional traits vary as a child develops, and that these traits are malleable and can be modified by focused interventions. The vignettes of Edward and Alyssa illustrate the two competing caricatures of gifted students, with Alyssa representing the well-adjusted gifted child and Edward representing the vulnerable gifted child. The vignette of Ms. Alvarez and Mr. Johnson depicts several of the recommended features of a social and emotional curriculum appropriate for gifted students. In closing, a vignette of a third child named Sally — a child who displays a range of social and emotional strengths and vulnerabilities — is developed to illuminate psychosocial traits of a student who, like many gifted students, fits into neither stereotype.

Meet Sally

Sally is an eighth-grade student at ECMS. Sally was selected for inclusion in the ECMS gifted program based on her creative talents in writing and her ability and achievement test scores, most of which were above the 90th percentile.

Sally has always "marched to the beat of her own drum." She loves to write detailed stories and poems about utopian and dystopian worlds. In fact, she won the ECMS creative writing award for one of her stories in seventh grade. She also loves history because she imagines herself as characters — a lady in waiting, a runaway slave, a hippie — inhabiting a variety of historical periods. In contrast to her writing and creative talents, Sally struggles in math and lacks self-esteem in this area. Her difficulty in math frequently frustrates her, and she needs the encouragement of her parents and math teacher to complete her homework and persevere in keeping up.

Three years ago, Sally's parents divorced after several years of intense arguing. Sally lost interest in school for several months following the separation of her parents. She also frequently became emotionally overwhelmed. However, after family counseling, Sally's parents have made strides in eliminating hostility in front of Sally. Since then, Sally's emotional overwhelm has diminished and she has regained her academic motivation, particularly as she has grown accustomed to splitting time with her parents.

Most of Sally's peers and teachers think she is "quirky" and excessively talkative. However, her art and language arts teachers enjoy the creativity she brings to these classes. Moreover, Ms. Alvarez recognizes her creative gifts and appreciates her high level of sensitivity when her history class discusses historically difficult topics such as slavery. Sally often joins the bibliotherapy group lunches that are held each week. Following her parents' divorce, she used her poetry writing as a mechanism for addressing the sadness she felt. Sally has had two best friends since kindergarten who share her love of fantasy and story-telling. They are inseparable. Although Sally recognizes that she is not one of the more "popular" students at school; she is happy with having two friends and with the nature of her friendships. Sally's parents used to pressure her to be more social and join more clubs. Ultimately, they came to realize that Sally preferred having her two best friends and being a little quirky. Sally's parents still worry about her tendency to get emotionally overwhelmed at what she considers to be societal injustices, such as global refugee crises and cruelty to animals. This summer, Mr. Johnson and Ms. Alvarez found a mentor from the local Red Cross who is letting her do an internship. Her parents have also started taking Sally to the Society for the Prevention of Cruelty to Animals on Saturdays so that she can help care for the animals.

The vignette of Sally illustrates the broad range of social and emotional strengths and weaknesses experienced by many, indeed most, gifted children. Sally is neither the most well-liked student at school nor one who is socially isolated. She enjoys strong and supportive relationships with some, but not all, of her teachers. Moreover, Sally's academic motivation and self-efficacy varies by subject and they are impacted by emotional challenges at home. However, because motivation and self-efficacy — like many psychosocial correlates — are developmental, Sally benefits from targeted counseling and affective curriculum interventions. As such, this vignette of Sally offers a more balanced view of the social and emotional characteristics of a "typical" gifted student, and belies the stereotypic conceptions held by many that gifted children are either exceptionally well-adjusted emotionally and successful socially or socially isolated and emotionally maladjusted.

ENDNOTES

[1] Subotnik, R. F., Olszewski-Kubilius, P., & Worrell, F. C. (2011). Rethinking giftedness and gifted education: A proposed direction forward based on psychological science. Psychological Science in the Public Interest, 12, 3-54.

[2] Terman, L. M. (1925/1947). Genetic studies of genius. Stanford, CA: Stanford University Press.

[3] Martin, L. T., Burns, R. M., & Schonlau, M. (2009). Mental disorders among gifted and nongifted youth: A selected review of the epidemiologic literature. Gifted Child Quarterly, 54, 31-41.

[4] For more information about self-concept, self-efficacy, and self-esteem, see Matthews, M. S. (2014). Self-concept and the gifted. In J. A. Plucker & C. M. Callahan (Eds.), Critical issues and practices in gifted education: What the research says (2nd ed., pp. 567-575). Waco, TX: Prufrock Press and Subotnik, R. F., Olszewski Kubilius, P., & Worrell, F. C. (2011). Rethinking giftedness and gifted education: A proposed direction forward based on psychological science. Psychological Science in the Public Interest, 12, 3-54.

[5] VanTassel-Baska, J. L., Cross, T. L., & Olenchak, F. R. (Eds.). (2009). Social-Emotional curriculum with gifted and talented students. Waco, TX: Prufrock Press.

[6] A good summary of research on motivation can be found in Clinkenbeard, P. R. (2014). Motivation and goals. In J. A. Plucker & C. M. Callahan (Eds.), Critical issues and practices in gifted education: What the research says (2nd ed., pp. 427-437). Waco, TX: Prufrock Press.

[7] Mueller, C. E. (2009). Protective factors as barriers to depression in gifted and nongifted adolescents. Gifted Child Quarterly, 53, 3-14.

[8] Rudasill, K. M., Adelson, J. L., Callahan, C. M., Houlihan, D. V., & Keizer, B. M. (2012). Gifted students' perceptions of parenting styles: Association with cognitive ability, sex, race and age. Gifted Child Quarterly, 57, 15-24.

[9] Gentry, M. Steenbergen-Hu, S, & Choi, B. (2011). Student-identified exemplary teachers: Insights from talented teachers. Gifted Child Quarterly, 55, 111-125.

[10] Robinson, A. (2014). Teacher characteristics and high-ability learners. In J. A. Plucker & C. M. Callahan (Eds.), Critical practices and issues and practices in gifted education: What the research says (2nd ed., pp. 645-658). Waco, TX: Prufrock Press.

[11] National Association for Gifted Children. (2010). NAGC pre-K-grade 12 gifted programming standards: A blueprint for quality gifted education programs. Retrieved from http://www.nagc.org

[12] See, e.g., Colangelo, N., Assouline, S., & Gross, M. U. M. (2004). A nation deceived: How schools hold back America's brightest students (Vols. I & II). Iowa City: University of Iowa, Belin-Blank International Center for Gifted Education and Talent Development, and Hertberg-Davis, H., & Callahan, C. M. (2014). Advanced Placement and International Baccalaureate Programs. In J. A. Plucker & C. M. Callahan (Eds.), Critical issues and practices in gifted education: What the research says (2nd ed., pp. 47-63). Waco, TX: Prufrock Press.

[13] Bain, S. K., & Bell, S. M. (2014). Social self-concept, social attributions, and peer relationships in fourth, fifth and sixth graders who are gifted compared to high achievers. Gifted Child Quarterly, 58, 167-178.

[14] A good summary of research on gender issues can be found in Callahan, C. M., & Hébert, T. P. (2014). Gender issues. In J. A. Plucker & C. M. Callahan (Eds.), Critical issues and practices in gifted education: What the research says (2nd ed., pp. 267-280). Waco, TX: Prufrock Press.

[15] Gross, M. U. M. (2004). Exceptionally gifted children (2nd ed.). London, England: Routledge Farmer.

[16] Silverman, L. K. (1997). The construct of asynchronous development. Peabody Journal of Education, 72, 36-58.

[17] Two good summaries of the BFLPE can be found in Matthews, M. S. (2014). Self-concept and the gifted. In J. A. Plucker & C. M. Callahan (Eds.), Critical issues and practices in gifted education: What the research says (2nd ed., pp. 567-575). Waco, TX: Prufrock Press, and Dai, D. Y., Rinn, A. N., & Tan, X. (2013). When the big fish turns small: Effects of participating in gifted summer programs on academic self-concepts. Journal of Advanced Academics, 24, 4-26.

[18] Callahan, C. M., & Hébert, T. P. (2014). Gender issues. In J. A. Plucker & C. M. Callahan (Eds.), Critical issues and practices in gifted education: What the research says (2nd ed., pp. 267-280). Waco, TX: Prufrock Press.

[19] Assouline, S. G., Colangelo, N., & Heo, N. (2014). Counseling gifted and talented students. In J. A. Plucker & C. M. Callahan (Eds.), Critical issues and practices in gifted education: What the research says (2nd ed., pp. 159-172). Waco, TX: Prufrock Press.

[20] Worrell, F. C. (2014). Ethnically diverse students. In J. A. Plucker & C. M. Callahan (Eds.), Critical practices and issues and practices in gifted education: What the research says (2nd ed., pp. 237-254). Waco, TX: Prufrock Press, and Worrell, F. C. (2007). Ethnic identity, academic achievement, and global self-concept in four groups of academically talented adolescents. Gifted Child Quarterly, 51, 23-38.

[21] Dweck, C. (2006). Mindset: The new psychology of success. New York, NY: Random House.

[22] Silverman, L. K. (2007). Perfectionism: The crucible of giftedness. Gifted Education International, 23, 233-245.

[23] Robinson, A. (2014). Teacher characteristics and high-ability learners. In J. A. Plucker & C. M. Callahan (Eds.), Critical practices and issues and practices in gifted education: What the research says (2nd ed., pp. 645-658). Waco, TX: Prufrock Press.

[24] National Association for Gifted Children. (2010). NAGC pre-K-grade 12 gifted programming standards: A blueprint for quality gifted education programs. Retrieved from http://www.nagc.org

[25] Worrell, F. C. (2014). Ethnically diverse students. In J. A. Plucker & C. M. Callahan (Eds.), Critical practices and issues and practices in gifted education: What the research says (2nd ed., pp. 237-254). Waco, TX: Prufrock Press, and Worrell, F. C. (2007). Ethnic identity, academic achievement, and global self-concept in four groups of academically talented adolescents. Gifted Child Quarterly, 51, 23-38.

[26] Nicpon, M. F., Rickels, H., Assouline, S. G., & Richards, A. (2012). Self-esteem and self-concept examination among gifted students with ADHD. Journal for the Education of the Gifted, 35, 220-240.

[27] Antshel, K. M., Faraone, S. V., Maglione, K., Doyle, A., Fried, R., Seidman, L., & Biederman, J. (2008). Temporal stability of

ADHD in the high-IQ population: Results from the MGH Longitudinal Family Studies of ADHD. Journal of American Academy of Child and Adolescent Psychiatry, 47, 817-825.

[28] Nicpon, M. F., Rickels, H., Assouline, S. G., & Richards, A. (2012). Self-esteem and self-concept examination among gifted students with ADHD. Journal for the Education of the Gifted, 35, 220-240.

[29] Subotnik, R. F., Olszewski-Kubilius, P., & Worrell, F. C. (2011). Rethinking giftedness and gifted education: A proposed direction forward based on psychological science. Psychological Science in the Public Interest, 12, 3-54.

[30] Nicpon, M. F., & Pfeiffer, S. I. (2011). High ability students: New ways to conceptualize giftedness and provide psychological services in the schools. Journal of Applied Psychology, 27, 293-305.

[31] VanTassel-Baska, J. L., Cross, T. L., & Olenchak, F. R. (Eds.). (2009). Social-Emotional curriculum with gifted and talented students. Waco, TX: Prufrock Press.

[32] Colangelo, N., Assouline, S., & Gross, M. U. M. (2004). A nation deceived: How schools hold back America's brightest students (Vols. I & II). Iowa City: University of Iowa, the Belin-Blank International Center for Gifted Education and Talent Development.

[33] Hertberg-Davis, H., & Callahan, C. M. (2014). Advanced Placement and International Baccalaureate Programs. In J. A. Plucker & C. M. Callahan (Eds.), Critical issues and practices in gifted education: What the research says (2nd ed., pp. 47-63). Waco, TX: Prufrock Press.

[34] See, e.g., Peterson, J. S., Getts, G., & Bradley, T. (2009). Discussion groups as a component of affective curriculum for gifted students. In J. L. VanTassel-Baska, J. L. Cross, & F. R. Olenchak (Eds.), Social-emotional curriculum with gifted and talented students (pp. 289-320). Waco, TX: Prufrock Press.

[35] Renzulli, J. S., Koehler, J., & Fogarty, E. (2006). Operation Houndstooth intervention theory: Social capital in today's schools. Gifted Child Today, 29, 14-24.

[36] VanTassel-Baska, J. L. (2009). Affective curriculum and instruction for gifted learners. In J. L. VanTassel-Baska, T. L. Cross, & F. R. Olenchak (Eds.), Social-emotional curriculum with gifted and talented students (pp 113-132). Waco, TX: Prufrock Press.

KEY RESOURCES FOR PARENTS AND EDUCATORS

For in-depth coverage of multiple issues relating to the emotional and social traits and needs of gifted students: Callahan, C. M., & Hertberg-Davis, H. (Eds.). (2013). *Fundamentals of gifted education: Considering multiple perspectives*. New York, NY: Routledge.

For an examination of the positive educational, emotional, and social impacts of acceleration and ability grouping for gifted students: Colangelo, N., Assouline, S., & Gross, M. U. M. (2004). *A nation deceived: How schools hold back America's brightest students* (Vols. I & II). Iowa City: University of Iowa, the Belin-Blank International Center for Gifted Education and Talent Development. http://www.accelerationinstitute.org/nation_deceived/get_report.aspx

For information concerning a counseling framework useful to school psychologists working with gifted children: Nicpon, M. F., & Pfeiffer, S. I. (2011). High ability students: New ways to conceptualize giftedness and provide psychological services in the schools. *Journal of Applied Psychology, 27*, 293-305.

For in-depth information providing a basis for policies, rules, and procedures that are essential for providing systematic programs and services to gifted students: National Association for Gifted Children (2010). *NAGC pre-K-grade 12 gifted programming standards: A blueprint for quality gifted education programs.* Washington, DC: Author. www.nagc.org

For a comprehensive review of the psychosocial variables associated with giftedness:

Subotnik, R. F., Olszewski-Kubilius, P., & Worrell, F. C. (2011). Rethinking giftedness and gifted education: A proposed direction forward based on psychological science. *Psychological Science in the Public Interest, 12*, 3-54.

For in-depth coverage of multiple issues relating to the emotional and social traits and needs of gifted students: Plucker, J. A., & Callahan, C. M. (Eds.). (2014). *Critical issues and practices in gifted education: What the research says* (2nd ed). Waco, TX: Prufrock Press.

For a broad examination of several affective curricula for gifted students: VanTassel-Baska, J. L., Cross, T. L., & Olenchak, F. R. (Eds.). (2009). *Social-Emotional curriculum with gifted and talented students*. Waco, TX: Prufrock Press.

ABOUT THE AUTHOR

Tracy C. Missett, Ph.D., is an assistant professor in the Department of Education at Sweet Briar College, and an adjunct faculty member teaching graduated gifted education courses at Marshall University. She holds a bachelor's degree in Rhetoric and Communications Studies from the University of Virginia, a law degree from the University of California, Hastings College of the Law, a Master of Arts degree in education from Teachers College, Columbia University, and a Ph.D. in Educational Psychology from the University of Virginia. Her research interests include twice-exceptional, particularly those with complex emotional profiles, and creativity as a component of giftedness.

ABOUT THE SERIES EDITOR

Cheryll M. Adams, Ph.D., is the Director Emerita of the Center for Gifted Studies and Talent Development at Ball State University. She has served on the Board of Directors of NAGC and has been president of the Indiana Association for the Gifted and the Association for the Gifted, Council for Exceptional Children.

65365594R00031

Made in the USA
Lexington, KY
10 July 2017